How to Start a Money Making Blog: The Best Methods, Tricks and Steps for Successful and Profitable Blogging

John Roberts

www.underpaidoverworked.com

Facebook: https://www.facebook.com/jroberts444

Copyright @ 2019

All Rights Reserved

ISBN: 9781798553701

Title: **How to Start a Money Making Blog:** The Best Methods, Tricks and Steps for Successful and Profitable Blogging

Author: John Roberts

www.underpaidoverworked.com

Text Copyright © JOHN ROBERTS

All rights reserved. No part of this guide may be reproduced in any form without permission in writing from the publisher except in the case of brief quotations embodied in critical articles or reviews.

Legal & Disclaimer

The information contained in this book and its contents is not designed to replace or take the place of any form professional advice; and is not meant to replace the need for independent professional advice or services, as may be required. The content and information in this book has been provided for educational and entertainment purposes only.

The content and information contained in this book has been compiled from sources deemed reliable, and it is accurate to the best of the Author's knowledge, information and belief. However, the Author cannot guarantee its accuracy and validity and cannot be held liable for any errors and/or omissions. Further, changes are periodically made to this book as and when needed. Where appropriate and/or necessary, you must consult a professional before using any of the suggested remedies, techniques, or information in this book.

Upon using the contents and information contained in this book, you agree to hold harmless the Author from and against any damages, costs, and expenses, including any legal fees potentially resulting from the application of any of the information provided by this book. This disclaimer applies to any loss, damages or injury caused by the use and application, whether directly or indirectly, of any advice or information presented, whether for breach of contract, tort, negligence, personal injury, criminal intent, or under any other cause of action.

You agree to accept all risks of using the information presented inside this book.

You agree that by continuing to read this book, where appropriate and/or necessary, you shall consult a before using any of the suggested remedies, techniques, or information in this book.

Table Of Contents

The Best Methods, Tricks and Steps for Successful and Profitable Blogging.

Introduction

Vision
What goal(s) do you have?
What drives you?
Do you want to make money blogging?
If you're trying to make money, how much do you want/need to make?
What do you hope to gain from your blog?
What are your specific financial goals?
What are your specific traffic goals?

Purpose
Why do you want to blog?
Why do you want to build a platform?
Have you ever blogged before?
How can you envision this blog helping others?
What are your long-term aspirations?
What about your chosen topic makes you "hungry?"
Do you have any particular life experiences that will help you?
What is your story? Be concise.

Strategy
Who is your ideal reader?
What does your ideal reader want from you?
What kinds of things does your ideal reader purchase?
Where do they currently buy the things they want and need?
What makes them want to buy?
How do you expect to gain traffic?

If you expect to earn organic traffic, what avenues will you use?

If you are willing to pay for traffic, what methods will you use?

How much money are you willing and/or able to spend on your site?

Making Money Through Advertising on Your Blog

What You Need to Consider Before Joining an Ad Network

How to Sell More Sidebar Ads

Using Advertising on your Blog
- AdSense
- Register your website with AdSense advertising
- Create an ad or link ad unit in AdSense
- Copy the code of the ad unit and paste in your desired location in your website
- Check if your ads are running

Important Terms and Concepts in Advertising
- Impressions
- Clicks and Cost-per-click
- Click-through rates

Earning With Affiliate Marketing

Finding an affiliate link for your content

Creating the right type of content

General Affiliate Networks

Shopping/E-commerce Affiliate Networks

Company-level Affiliate Programs

How to Maximize Your Earning Potential Through Affiliate Marketing

Monetizing Your Blog Through Coaching Services

Why Coaching and How Can It Make Money for My Blog?

How to Get Started with Coaching on Your Blog

The Importance of Content Delivery

The Right Way to Deliver Content on Your Blog for Maximum Earning Potential

Monetizing Through Sponsored Posts

What Is the Earning Potential with Sponsored Content?

Why Sponsored Posts Are an Awesome Revenue Generating Tool

How to Secure Sponsored Posts on Your Blog

The Types of Sponsored Post Options to Work With

Monetizing Through Product Creation

Creating and Selling Online Courses

Selling Products, Services and Organizing Giveaways

Research

Writing, formatting and design

Marketing

So what did we learn on our travels?

Secrets for Creating and Rewriting Great Content

Content Curation

4 Ways for Finding Great Content in Your Niche

Free Photo Resources

9 Kick-Ass Resources to Enhance Your Content Writing from Good to Wow

Content Scheduling

How to Schedule Posts on WordPress

Introduction

Vision

Your vision for this venture is going to define what problem you are trying to solve. The vision statement of your blog might be your statement of faith, your "how to change the world" mantra, your idea for a better tomorrow; etc.

Usually the vision statement is a honed, specific, and idealistic set of virtues and morals that bind and guide an organization. For your site, it's not necessarily important to have such a lengthy, in-depth analysis of your overall vision, but it is important to outline a brief set of ideals.

Use your best judgment for length—this "statement" isn't going to be publicized; it's for your own use. However, if you keep it short, it might be something that you can print

What goal(s) do you have?

WHAT GOAL(S) do you have?

The first step in tackling a project of any size isn't writing strategies, tactics, and quantitative goals.

Instead, the first step is going to be brainstorming. That's it—just brainstorm the types of things you don't get to brainstorm about normally: Dreams, aspirations, etc. Just spend a few minutes daydreaming about your life, and what you imagine perfect would be like.

Your goals—daydreams—are going to help define the answers to the following 100 questions, and these "life goals" are things we're going to try to fit into your ideal image of blogging. Don't worry about holding back or being unrealistic; there's plenty of time for that later!

Blogging can fit nicely into your world and be a fun hobby, or it can change your life. The choice is yours; and now it's time to figure out just how to make your dreams come true!

What drives you?

WHAT DRIVES YOU?

This is the "million-dollar question" about blogging, and sometimes about life in general.

What makes you "hungry"?

You must know what drives you to succeed; what you will wake up early for and go to bed late for. Answer this question, as honestly and genuinely as possible—of the many questions in this book, this question is one of the few that you won't be able to "Google" the answer to.

Be

Do you want to make money blogging?

DO YOU WANT to make money blogging?

Is this a side project that "might turn into something," or is it going to be a muse that provides you with a lifestyle change?

To some people, this is a strange question. "Of course," they say, "why wouldn't I want to make money?"

The answer, though, is different for everyone. Sometimes people just want to have an outlet for their rants, political musings, or artistic whims. That's fine.

But many other people go into blogging and Internet marketing to make money. There's nothing wrong with that, but you need to be aware of the difficulties and struggles inherent with starting a profitable blog.

If you're trying to make money, how much do you want/need to make?

IF YOU'RE TRYING to make money, how much do you want/need to make?

In terms of annual income, do you hope this site will make you rich, offer a steady side income, or replace your current salary? Be specific, meaning write out the actual amounts!

Again, you might not need to make money, but it wouldn't hurt.

Or you might despise the concept of blogging for profits.

Finally, this blog might be your "lifelong dream," providing you with an escape route from your normal 9-5. No matter what it is, though, be specific about what you need per year financially.

What do you hope to gain from your blog?

WHAT DO YOU hope to gain from your blog?

Not every site needs to generate income, but you do need to have a specific reason you're doing it. Here are a few specific examples:

"To replace or supplement my current annual income."

"I like the feeling I get when someone thanks me for what I'm doing."

"To provide a public forum for debating current issues."

"To learn from sharing and connecting with others, and possibly earn income on the side."

What are your specific financial goals?

WHAT ARE YOUR specific financial goals?

What do you hope your blog will earn in a year? Write your goals (not yet projections—that comes later) below.

6-Month:

9-Month:

12-Month:

These numbers don't have to be based on anything other than speculation—as we continue through these questions, you'll start to develop a better understanding of what you can accomplish with a blog, and you can write updated answers in your final business plan.

What are your specific traffic goals?

WHAT ARE YOUR specific traffic goals?

How many visitors do you hope to have at each of these checkpoints? A "site visitor" is a measurable statistic that tracks actual human visitors to a website or blog. Usually these measurements are taken over a 30-day continuous period.

For the following time periods, you're asking yourself what you hope your trailing 30-day average will be upon reaching these checkpoints.

Same thing as before, though: don't worry about being accurate or realistic if you have no idea. Just write something. We'll go more into what good traffic numbers should be as we answer more questions.

6-Month:

9-Month:

12-Month:

Purpose

This is the point in the book when you'll start to analyze your specific purpose for blogging.

For some people it's as simple as making more money.

For many others, it's about creating something from nothing, and leaving behind a legacy.

Chances are, you've already got a good idea of your purpose for blogging or writing—this section is just going to help you iron out the details and get a clearer picture of the end goal.

As always, answer these questions as honestly and genuinely as possible—and be sure to

Why do you want to blog?

WHY DO YOU want to blog?

Blogging is different than having a blog. Many people know they'd like to have a successful blog, but sometimes forget that it takes a successful blogger to build that blog.

Previously, you were asked if you'd like to make money from your blog. Here, you can expound on that answer—if you want to make money, why?

If you want to be more respected or recognized in a certain field, why do you want to do it by blogging?

This is probably one of the hardest questions to answer, since it's not vision-based. Vision-based questions lead us to lofty, idealistic "perfect-case" scenarios, whereas this question is asking more of a "down and dirty" question: What is it about blogging that you love/like/appreciate?

Why do you want to build a platform?

WHY DO YOU want to build a platform?

What benefit do you have to offer others?

Building a platform is a great way to get your message into the world, but why does your message need to be there in the first place? Are you trying to improve humanity? Save the hungry? Preach the Gospel?

Whatever it is, it's there. There's a particular reason you want to get your message out to thousands (and yes, it can be just about the money).

Write it down.

Have you ever blogged before?

HAVE YOU EVER blogged before?

What writing or blogging experience will you draw from if you start a blog?

Some people have heard that blogging is easy—that may be true in it's simplicity.

But what about getting people to pay attention to you, or getting people to find you in the first place?

What about dealing with the many emails, comments, and technical work related to maintaining a growing blog?

Write out

How can you envision this blog helping others?

HOW CAN YOU envision this blog helping others?

Making money online is great reason to start a blog, but without a passion for interacting and helping others, it might quickly be a cause of burnout for you. Many bloggers don't even care about making money—they just want to help people.

At its core, blogging was birthed from a "personal diary"-style of helping and interacting with others. People are searching for answers to their questions online, and bloggers are there to greet them, offering a (hopeful) solution or answer.

What is your solution going to be?

What are your long-term aspirations?

WHAT ARE YOUR long-term aspirations?

Blogs can grow and adapt into much more than just an anecdotal website.

If you're trying to make money, are you going to plan to grow the blog into a larger service-based website? Will you build a blog in one niche, then another, hoping to sell each as they start to grow?

Is the blog the entire business model? Will you eventually grow into providing offline services?

Answer the above questions as well as you can, and you'll start to see what your

What about your chosen topic makes you "hungry?"

WHAT ABOUT YOUR chosen topic makes you "hungry?"

Above, you answered the "million-dollar question" about blogging—"what makes you hungry?" This time, answer why that topic makes you hungry for more.

The hunger level you have regarding this topic is crucial to building a self-sustaining enterprise online. You either need to love the idea of building a blog for awhile, then selling it to someone else or hiring someone to write for you, or you need to love the

Do you have any particular life experiences that will help you?

DO YOU HAVE any particular life experiences that will help you?

What are some of your life experiences that will help you create content for your topic.

List as many character-building points here. Also, having a "story" will help you interact, engage, and connect with your future readers. People are drawn to stories—whether they're fiction-based or well-told nonfiction.

Start thinking about your particular story, and why it's compelling enough to draw

What is your story? Be concise.

WHAT IS YOUR story? Be concise.

This is the basic foundation of your "About" page, and possibly the blurb that will show up on your sidebar—be brief, but personable.

Check out the blogs you read most often, and look through their "About" pages. You'll see that many of them tell a story; it's personal, down-to-earth, and real.

Your story needs to engage and draw in your readers, but it needs to be concise.

As Alfred Hitchcock said, "a story is life with the boring parts left out."

Strategy

First, any strong and successful business has a defined Vision Statement and Purpose. These statements are ideal-based, rather than quantitative, but they're statements that project the overall message of the business.

Your Vision and Purpose will likewise explain to people at a subconscious level what your blog is all about—the things you stand for, believe in, and want others to know about you.

Second, starting with Strategy and Structure is a recipe for disaster at worst, and leads to confusion at best.

Ask any professional or well-seasoned veteran blogger how many times they struggled trying to get the best theme or the coolest plugins installed on their site, and how much time they estimate they've wasted on trivial things, like neat-looking social media icons.

Their current design and layout wasn't reached at random, by fiddling until it was "just right." They stepped back and looked at their Purpose for blogging and their personal Vision for their blogging lifestyle, and built the structural components of their site accordingly.

You've done the same by focusing on those two aspects first, rather than two years down the road!

Who is your ideal reader?

WHO IS YOUR ideal reader?

Finding your ideal—or "perfect"—reader is paramount to developing a consistent and targeted branding identity.

You'll need to know who your "ideal reader" is before you start writing, unless you're only writing for yourself.

When clarifying your ideal reader, be as specific as possible—give them a name, identity, a job, and a family (if they have one...). Give them a face and body type, and a gender. You want to have a very specific idea of whom you're trying to target.

Here's a hint: Start by describing yourself!

What does your ideal reader want from you?

WHAT DOES YOUR ideal reader want from you?

What one question are they asking that they want you to answer?

If you don't know what they're asking, you can further refine your ideal reader or you can start looking online for questions. Seek out the websites and forums they're using and reading (which ones are you reading?), and browse through the questions and answers they're writing about.

What kinds of things does your ideal reader purchase?

WHAT KINDS OF things does your ideal reader purchase?

What do they buy that they need (staples—food, clothing, etc.) and what do they want to buy?

If you're blogging about an improved staple (a "better mousetrap," if you will), you're going to have the benefit of not needing to talk people into why they need your product (they already use it). However, you're going to have to figure out how to make a staple product (a lamp, macaroni and cheese, tires, etc.) noteworthy enough to write about over and over again.

On the other hand, products and services that are new to the general public or your target market are going to be easier to write about, but it will be harder to convince others of their necessity (and why they should buy from you).

Figure out what kinds of purchases your ideal reader makes, and craft your blogging message to their interests and needs.

Where do they currently buy the things they want and need?

WHERE DO THEY currently buy the things they want and need?

Are they an Amazon shopper, or a boutique shopper?

Most people are price-conscious, but a segment of online shoppers are just looking for the absolute best, regardless of cost.

If you can convince your readers that you not only have the best offering, for the best price, they might buy from you. One of the things bloggers forget, though, is that it's not just the product quality and price that people are conscious of, but the reputation of the site.

They'll buy from you only if your blog or website looks worthy enough of their business. Amazon has a proven track record of sales and customer satisfaction, and no one will argue that they're going to take your money.

Convince your readers on a subconscious level that your site is reputable and ready for business through design, layout, and security.

What makes them want to buy?

WHAT MAKES THEM want to buy?

Everyone's an impulse buyer when it comes to certain things—what makes your ideal reader purchase on the spot? In fact, what makes you purchase something immediately?

Think about grocery check out lines—magazines, gum, candy, energy drinks—all of these things speak to the inner subconscious of the consumer: "Oh yeah, I do need to know what's going on with that celebrity wedding!"

What about your blog—your product—will make people buy (read) what you have to say? Is it a promise of something better? The opportunity to learn from your expertise? A personal account, told in an amazingly fresh way?

Think about this question, and write some possibilities—there probably aren't any wrong answers, which makes it all the harder to do. But the longer you analyze these

How do you expect to gain traffic?

HOW DO YOU expect to gain traffic?

Traffic is crucial to a successful blog, unless your definition of success is having a site no one visits.

You need to start thinking about the ways you'll attempt to direct readers to your blog, long before you start one. Do you have a preexisting platform or professional persona that will allow you to attract attention quickly? Are you going to run ads, pay for traffic, or hold giveaways?

One of the best ways to gain free, targeted, and engaged traffic is through a strategy called "guest-posting." The idea is that you'll write articles and blog posts for other sites, submitting to larger blogs in your niche. It's a strategy many bloggers (including me!) have used to grow very quickly, and all it costs is time.

Used in conjunction with other traffic-generation methods can exponentially enhance your efforts, though, so start thinking about it now!

If you expect to earn organic traffic, what avenues will you use?

IF YOU EXPECT to earn organic traffic, what avenues will you use?

Organic traffic is traffic that you don't pay for. Social media, newsletter subscriptions, SEO, links, forums, guest-posting, etc. are all examples of organic traffic sources, and it's usually agreed that organic traffic is stronger (in the sense that it often delivers more engaged readers) than non-organic traffic.

You should definitely strive to increase your ability to earn organic traffic as much as possible. Start leaving helpful and insightful comments on sites in your niche (more on this later), and visit and join any forums where like-minded people gather and discuss your topic(s).

These are long-term strategies, where consistency and relevance add the most value. Don't expect to generate massive amounts of traffic to your site overnight, but instead let your organic traffic strategies add up and eventually cause a "snowball" of great traffic to your blog.

If you are willing to pay for traffic, what methods will you use?

IF YOU ARE willing to pay for traffic, what methods will you use?

As you know by now, organic traffic isn't the only kind of traffic you can generate to your website.

You can buy advertisements through Google's AdSense program, BuySellAds, Chitika, or other marketplaces, or you can buy sponsored forum/blog posts, pay for guest articles and blog posts on other websites.

These aren't bad strategies at all—just be sure to have a great-looking and useful website ready for visitors when you start buying ads

How much money are you willing and/or able to spend on your site?

HOW MUCH MONEY are you willing and/or able to spend on your site?

If you plan to engage in non-organic traffic generation methods like purchasing ads, start thinking about your overall daily/weekly/bi-weekly ad budget.

Write down the amount of money you can safely spend on advertisements for your site:

- Per week?

- Per month?

- Per year?

Many bloggers feel that sticking to a set schedule, for a set period of time, is the best way to gain from ads. Make sure you're able to spend the same amount of money for at least 1-2 months in a particular advertising stream, and preferably 6-8 months or longer. Remember, you need to drive traffic to a site that's ready to receive traffic, so before you go out and purchase $1,000 of ads, read through the next few sections of this book!

Making Money Through Advertising on Your Blog

Monetizing your blog is going to require quite a bit of effort, and one of the ways to generate an income is through advertising. Advertising here can include sidebar ads, in addition to your average standard ad that you see on blogs which are already making money.

What You Need to Consider Before Joining an Ad Network

There is only one reason you would join an ad network – to make money, of course. But before you go jumping into all sorts of ad networks in an attempt to make the most money out of your blog, there are a couple of things which you are going to need to consider here:

Will the ad network be able to offer you the guaranteed CPM rate you are after? Be mindful of the fact that many ad networks are guilty of enticing new or struggling bloggers with promises of great returns, but remember that if an offer sounds too good to be true, then it probably is.

Do you have a contract? An agreement in black and white is always the way to go, and if an ad network is reluctant to offer you a concrete agreement, best to walk away from it to avoid finding yourself getting stuck in a bad situation.

Will you have any sort of control over the ads that are run? Ideally, the ads that are going to be featured on your blog should be in sync with the content that is being talked about on your blog. You do not want an ad that is in contrast to your content because it is going to send mixed messages to your readers and your blog runs the risk of losing credibility among your followers. When signing up with an ad network, get it in writing that you have the right to request any ads you deem inappropriate for your blog to be removed without issues.

Joining an ad network has its pros and cons. Ad networks basically work like advertising brokers, whereby you offer an available advertising space on your blog for purchase, and they will do their part trying to sell the space for you for a cut of the sale.

The pros of working with an ad network are:

There is less effort on your part in the sense that you are not stuck being a one-person show doing all the legwork selling and setting up your advertising. By joining an ad network, all you have to do is sign a contract and place an HTML code on your sidebar, and you are set.

Ad networks can sometimes earn more than private advertising can, although how much you make would vary depending on several factors.

Ad networks do more than just sell ads since they work with multiple bloggers and have more connections. They can attract a bigger pool of prospective clients, some of which may have big advertising budgets they can work with, an opportunity that may otherwise be harder to score if you were working on your own.

And now, the cons of working with an ad network:

You may not have as much control over the ads as you would like. Ad networks are often reluctant to relinquish control over the ads that get displayed to the blogger, although there are some exceptions. Do not work with an ad network unless you are prepared to give up control and let them have full run of the kind of advertisements that show up on your blog.

It may be difficult to secure an ad network to work with. Getting in with a network could require months of pushing and persistence. Having connections and contacts in this instance would definitely give you a leg up. Otherwise, it can be a challenge getting in immediately with these networks and very often you may find yourself waiting for months before an opportunity shows up.

How to Sell More Sidebar Ads

Average advertising is easy enough, and noticeable. It is the sidebar ads that very often go unnoticed in most blogs. But sidebar ads also have earning potential for your blog, so they should not be ignored. One great thing about selling sidebar ads is that you have complete control over the ads that get displayed on your blog at all times, which may not necessarily always be the case with regular advertising through an ad network.

So, how do you get the most out of your sidebar ads? By following these simple rules for monetization:

Emphasize on Making It Obvious – If an advertiser is looking to advertise on your blog, they may not notice that there is an option to advertise on your blog unless you make it loud and clear to them, plain and simple. Make it clear that you have advertising spots for sale by putting an advertisement tab in your header, for example, that will link advertisers to your advertising page. Remember a lot of these advertisers are most likely very busy people who simply do not have the time to comb and sift through your blog wondering if there is any advertising opportunity available. It is up to you to make it obvious.

Clarity on Your Advertising Page – Once you have directed advertisers to your advertisement page, make things even simpler for them by being as detailed as you possibly can. Typically, the kind of information that advertisers would be after include page views and unique visitors to your blog, what your blog's demographics are, and what are the advertising options and prices they can expect. And if you have any testimonials from former advertisers who have worked with you before? Even better! Throw that into the mix too, because it adds credibility to your blog. List down every compelling reason you can think of as to why advertisers should choose to work with you and you will be in business in no time.

Offer Special Rates – Nobody can resist a good discount or a bargain. If you want more advertisers to sign up with your sidebar ads, offer them a deal that they simply cannot refuse. For example, offer your sidebar advertising rates at 50% off the original price. Limited time offers are a great gimmick to entice these advertisers to sign up for your deal, and they will be a lot keener to take up a sidebar ad subscription on your blog if they feel that they are getting a bang for their buck.

Throw in an Extra Treat or Two – Companies love feeling like they are getting the most out of their money, and sidebar advertising is a great opportunity to make the companies who work with you feel special. Seal the deal with your new partners by offering to mention the company on your Facebook or Twitter accounts for example, which is a free form of publicity for the company. You could even offer to write a free blog post for the company if you love what they are selling and you are comfortable promoting their products or services to your readers.

Do not Leave Blank Spots – If your sidebar ads are empty, it gives the impression that your blog space is not quite up to par yet for people to want to advertise on your blog. This could be the kiss of death for your money generating attempts, so avoid leaving blank ad boxes even if you do not have any ad deals signed up. Fill those spots with affiliate ads or work with friends who run their own blogs and give them free advertising for example. Anything to keep up the appearance that your blog is interesting enough to advertise upon and this will, in turn, attract other advertisers if they see there is already an interest built on your blog.

Using Advertising on your Blog

Advertising is probably one of the earliest monetization practices and the easiest to implement in a website. If you have used the internet at least once in the past, there is no doubt that you have encountered an ad by Google or its alternatives in the market. These are examples of advertising networks. These networks facilitate the meeting of advertisers and publishers.

Google AdSense is probably the most popular and widely published advertising service in the world. Let's begin with this advertising tool:

AdSense

As mentioned in the previous parts of the book, AdSense is Google's ads publishing service for websites, YouTube videos, and apps. This advertising platform is one of the easiest to implement. To add it to your website, all you have to do is to follow these steps:

Register your website with AdSense advertising

The first challenge for using AdSense is getting your application approved. It is common for a website to have their application for access declined for various reasons. One of the most common reasons is the presence of banned content in your website.

AdSense cannot be used in websites that discuss topics like pornography, gambling or any other illegal activities. Even mentioning the word Baccarat once in your blog could trigger the anti-gambling flag of the registration process.

Fortunately, AdSense will show you the content in your website that prevented your registration from being approved. You will need to clean up your websites of all the mentioned content and resubmit it for reconsideration.

There are a lot of other reasons that a website's application is declined. It is also common for websites with low-quality content to be declined. If your web posts or pages only have a few sentences each, your application may also not go through. Just to make sure that your content is not flagged, make sure that each one contains at least 300 words.

Aside from these factors, the website's age may also be considered by the registration algorithm. If the blog is just a few days old, the AdSense team generally questions the commitment of the webmaster to stick with the project. This may lead them to halt the registration process until the website is at least a couple of weeks old and already has some content.

If this is the reason cited for your failure to register an account, then the best option is to keep creating content to populate your website. When AdSense detects that there is a steady increase of clean content for your website, it may allow you to post ads.

Create an ad or link ad unit in AdSense

After registration, the next step is to create ad units. By creating ad units, you will be able to name ads and adjust their appearance as they look in your website. Naming ads is important because the name will allow you to check which ad units are particularly effective in getting clicks.

You will have multiple options for ads in AdSense. You can create a simple banner ad. These banner ads have fixed sizes and are usually not suited for users using mobile phones. If your blog gets a lot of visits from mobile phone users, it may be best to use a responsive ad unit instead. Responsive ads adjust the size and shape of the ad container depending on the size of the screen of the users.

Aside from the above-mentioned ad formats, you can also create a link ad. Link ads differ from the two because they do not contain images. Instead, it only contains text links where in a list of topics is listed.

Native ad units are newer types of ads for AdSense publishers. This type of ad is also responsive. The key feature of this type of ad is that it is supposed to look like a part of your regular content. In the process of creating an ad unit, you will be asked to adjust the appearance of the ad. You will choose where the image of the ad will be shown. You may also modify the location and the color of the text in the ad.

The idea is to adjust these factors so that it looks like the ad is also a part of your content.

Copy the code of the ad unit and paste in your desired location in your website

After creating an ad unit, AdSense will show you a code that you will need to add the ad unit to your websites. To add ads to your website, you simply need to copy the code and paste it in the area where you want it to show.

The process on how to do this depends on the website management software that you are using. For WordPress users, for example, a number a plugin exists to help you insert your ads automatically into your website. You could make use of these plugins or you could add the ads manually.

Check if your ads are running

After creating your ad unit, it usually takes a few hours for it to be populated with the right kind of ads. If your account is new and your website has not been checked yet by the AdSense team, you may see some filler ads in the area where you placed the code.

After two to three hours, you should see ads already showing up in your chosen areas. The content of the ads are chosen based on an auction system. The advertisers set a maximum amount for bidding for ad places.

Every time a user requests a page with Google ads, the algorithm does an automatic auction for the ad spots in the page. The advertiser with the highest bid wins the spot. Their advertisement is shown in the spots where the codes are located.

Because of its simplicity and the popularity of Google ads, AdSense is one of the most used ads publishing service online. Almost all major news websites use AdSense. Because they are so common, AdSense has a reputation of having low click-through rates.

Now that we are discussing advertising, let us discuss some concepts that you may find useful when running ads to your business. Namely, let's talk about impressions, clicks, cost-per-click and click-through rates.

Important Terms and Concepts in Advertising

Impressions

Impressions refer to the accumulated number of times that visitors in your website load an ad on their screen. Let's say you have three ads in your post, one at the topmost part of your page (before the header), one within the content/article and one after the content.

When the page loads, the visitor only sees the topmost part of the web page. This imaginary line that divides the upper part of the page from the lower part is called 'the fold'. Everything above the fold is automatically seen by the visitor when the page loads.

Because one of your ads is located above the headers, we can safely assume that it is above the fold. Since the other two ads are in the content and after the content. They may be located below the fold.

An impression is only triggered when the visitor scrolls to the part where the ad is located. Once the page loads, all ads above the fold automatically ticks and adds to your impression count.

When the person scrolls down and reads the content, the other ads below the fold trigger an impression count. You will see the number of impressions for each ad unit in your AdSense Dashboard.

Clicks and Cost-per-click

As the name suggests, clicks refer to the number of times a visitor clicks on an ad in your webpage. Clicking an ad redirects the visitor to the advertiser's landing page. Most ads in the AdWords network pay via a cost-per-click system. That means that the advertiser only pays you when your visitors click on their ads.

Because you are only paid when ads are clicked, it is logical to think that your goals are basically to increase the number of clicks on the ads on your website. However, AdSense has strict rules in preventing fraudulent clicks.

From the AdSense point of view, a click is only valid if a person does it in his or her own choosing without being influenced by the content of the webpage to do so. Ideally, the person should really be interested in the advertising for the advertising network to be effective. However, this factor depends on the content of the ad and is beyond your control as the ad publisher.

Click-through rates

The click-through rates refer to the percentage of the time that visitors click on ads in your web pages compared to the total number of impressions. Let's say that you've shown a total of 1000 ads during an entire day to visitors. This is the total number of impressions for your website in the given timeline.

If 10 people clicked on ads, for example, you can get the click-through rates by dividing the number of clicks by the total number of impressions. This means that your click-through rate for that day is 0.01 or 1%.

It is common for AdSense publishers to have click-through rates south of 1%. This means that 99% of the ads viewed on the webpage has little to no value because they did not generate revenue for the blogger of the website owner. Because of this, most small time blogs choose to also find other means of monetizing their websites aside from their AdSense ads.

Earning With Affiliate Marketing

While advertising on your website is the easiest way to start, it is not the most profitable for most bloggers. People see blogs as a source of firsthand advice from writers who also went through the same issues. When people go to blogs for information, it is likely that the information that they are looking for cannot be found in other types of websites.

The most successful bloggers are skilled in gaining the trust of their readers. When their readers trust them enough, they are usually open to the suggestions of the blogger. This gives the word of the blogger some power in their own industry.

Let's say I have a blog about gardening. I have been maintaining the blog for years now. The comments section and the social media widgets on my blog show that I am followed by thousands of readers. The archive list on my sidebar also indicates that they have been active for years.

These are all trust factors that reinforce to a new visitor that I am a credible source. It increases the chances that my reader will trust my content. If these trust factors work, even new visitors may take my advice.

In my gardening blog, I provide free content on how to grow special types of plants. I also show pictures of the flowers and the vegetables that grow from my plants. I talk to the reader as if he or she was my friend.

In my instructional posts, I include a product or two that I actually use and a link that will lead the buyer where they can buy the product. This is where affiliate marketing comes in. When giving the readers links where they could buy the products I show in my posts, I use a link that comes from the affiliate account I created with the seller's website.

When the buyer clicks on the link, they are tracked by the seller's website. If they do make a purchase on the seller's website after clicking my link, then I am credited for the purchase. As a reward for facilitating a sale, I get a percentage of the purchase price. This percentage is called the commission rate.

Let's say that the person I referred to the seller's website spent $100 and the affiliate program has a 10% commission rate. This means that I will get 10% of the total amount spent. In this case, I will get $10 for a successful referral.

Finding an affiliate link for your content

There are thousands of affiliate links on the internet. However, you cannot just pick any affiliate program and post its links to your blog. Posting links alone will not get you any sales. To become a successful affiliate, you should match the product that you offer to your readers to the type of content that you are posting.

If you are posting about your take on the country's political events, for example, you should consider promoting political books to your readers. On the other hand, if you are blogging about your experience cooking at home, you should consider promoting appliances, cooking tools, and recipe books.

Aside from considering your topic and the type of content that you are offering, you should also consider the demographics of the readers of your blog. If you are posting content that is more appealing to men, find a product that also appeals to men.

Let's say you are blogging about the local professional sports team. Men usually buy the jerseys of the popular members of that team. You can post these affiliate marketing items on your website.

If your blog posts are mostly read by women, on the other hand, you will need to adjust the products that you are selling. You do not need to promote the most expensive product in the list of items of the seller. You are not aiming to actually suggest something that the readers may want to buy.

It is impossible to guess this. Instead, you should just include products that are more likely to make them click. When they click and enter the seller's website, they are no longer your responsibility. You should trust that the seller's website will be able to convert the traffic that you bring their way.

Creating the right type of content

Bloggers are basically content marketers. The content that you create in your website act as tools for catching people's attention. When people read, comment or share your content, we can say that they are engaging with your content. In the online marketing world, engagement is one of the most important metrics.

If you are reading this book, it is likely that you already have an idea of the types of people who visit your website. You may already know the types of content that get the most engagement. Most importantly, you should already know the reason why people go to your website.

Does your content make them laugh? Do you offer content that solves a problem? Does your website have special features that make them keep coming back?

Doing a simple survey in your blog also helps a lot if you are just starting out and you don't know who your website audience is. You can ask them their email address, their age, and their gender. This will allow you to learn the basic information of the people who visit your website.

You will be surprised by how different your expectations and the actual results are. Sometimes, a blogger expects that his viewers are mostly women, but their surveys show a mostly male audience. This also happens with much other demographic information.

Aside from creating a survey, you should also trust the statistics you gather from your blog. Most websites, for example, use Google Analytics and Google Webmaster tools for SEO. These tools are priceless when learning about your audience.

Both tools will help you learn where your viewers are from and how they reached your website (social, direct, organic search, referrals). These kinds of information are vital for the next step, which is creating the right type of content.

So let's first discuss the locations where your visitors are predominantly from. The best affiliate offers to put on your blog varies depending on the source country of your visitors. We will discuss Amazon affiliates later on because it is the easiest affiliate network to start and to make a profit from.

Amazon, however, will only be available for you if they have one in the country where your visitors are from. In most cases, you will not be able to create Amazon affiliate accounts non-English speaking countries. Amazon affiliate programs from these countries only allow websites using the country's native language to join.

The same goes with other affiliate networks. In CJ.com for example, each advertiser specifies their serviceable areas. If your visitors' country is not on the list, you will not gain anything by posting links of that advertiser on your blog.

The source/channel where your visitors came from is also an important factor to consider. Learning the sources gives you an idea of the intention of your visitor on your website. A visitor from the social networks, for example, is not as valuable as a visitor from search, when it comes to affiliate marketing.

Social networks are effective tools for gathering traffic. However, their users are not really looking for anything specific. They must have seen your link on Facebook or Twitter and it made them curious. They are looking to be entertained rather than to solve a problem.

In contrast, you want to attract more people who want to use your content to solve their problems. These people are more likely to click and buy from your affiliate links. Using Google Webmaster tools, you will also be able to learn more about the search information. The most important information here is the number of clicks that you get from search. Clicks basically mean traffic for your website.

However, aside from clicks, you can use this free tool for checking the position of your web pages in Google search. The position refers to the placement of your webpage in the Google search result page where your webpages appeared. Naturally, you want to rank 1st in all the major search terms in your niche market.

You may also be interested in the number of impressions that your websites are getting in Google search. Impressions refer to the number of times that your webpage was shown to searchers. This metric generally tells you the popularity of a search term among your prospect viewers.

Lastly, Google Webmaster tools give you some of the search terms used by potential visitors. This information is probably the most valuable for affiliate marketers. In general, you want your web pages to rank at a high position for search terms with a lot of impressions. By targeting these keywords, you will get more traffic to your website.

The Position column in Google webmaster tools, not only indicate your rank in the search pages, but also the amount of competition vying for the top spot. Successful affiliate marketers are experts at finding highly searched keywords with few competitors.

You will know if you have a lot of competition for a search term based on the number of impressions it gets and the average position of your pages with this particular phrase. Highly competitive search terms tend to put your newest content far from the first page.

A typical Google search results page contains 10 search results. If your average position for a search term is in the 50th position, this may mean that you are at the 5th page. People rarely venture this deep into the search results pages. It is highly unlikely for you to get any clicks on your website, this far from the front page.

Aside from these types of search terms, as an affiliate marketer, you should also try to target search terms that indicate intent to buy. Let's say you have a blog that talks about the newest gadgets in the market. A new product was just released in Amazon called, Product X. Gadget lovers are excited about

Product X and you managed to rank high in some keywords related to it:

The search term 'Product X photos' got you 200 website clicks and it is searched (impressions) for 3,000 times in the last 24 hours. You managed to rank 8th on this search term.

A second search term 'Product X review' is also gaining popularity at over 1,000 impressions. You are ranked 10th in this term and you got 10 clicks on this search term in the last 24 hours.

Lastly, you also managed to rank for 'Product X Discount Coupon'. This particular search term only ticked under 500 impressions in one day. Of the 500 impressions, only 3 clicked. You are ranked 12th for this search term.

If blogging was only a popularity contest, the logical approach would be to try to rank for content with more impressions. Most people would opt to optimize for the first search term 'Product X Photos'. As an affiliate marketer though, you want to attract visitors who actually want to buy the product you are promoting.

And so, based on the three search terms indicated above, the last search term, 'Product X Discount Coupon' shows the best intention to buy. Many people who are looking for discount coupons are already looking to buy the product and are just looking for a discount.

To increase your affiliate earnings, the best solution is to build a webpage that will rank well for this key phrase. For example, you could create a post with a list of the different online shops that offer discounts for Product X. You could also review

Product X and add a discount coupon for it somewhere in the review.

Types of Affiliate Marketing Programs

There are multiple types of affiliate marketing programs on the internet based on the way you classify each one. In this book, we will classify affiliate marketing programs based on the platform that offers them:

General Affiliate Networks

Affiliate networks refer to companies that offer a wide variety of affiliate marketing programs. These companies partner with advertisers. They also create a platform where ad publishers can sign up to a program, set up banner and text-link ad codes and monitor their progress. Rakuten Linkshare (now Rakuten Marketing) and CJ.com are two of the most popular of these types of affiliate marketing platforms.

In this type of platform, the blogger first needs to sign up with the network. This creates the first layer of quality checking for the network. In most of these networks, you will not be able to sign-up without a website. This protects the network from people who will just use the links to spam communities.

After signing up, the blogger needs to go through the available advertisers in the network. An affiliate network usually contains hundreds to even thousands of advertisers. The blogger needs to choose at least one that fits with his or her niche market.

After choosing the advertiser, the blogger needs to apply to their program. Most of the advertisers automatically accept affiliates. However, there are some companies who will screen the publisher first before doing so. This creates a second layer of quality control.

When screening, the advertisers usually check the volume of traffic that a website gets. While it is logical for advertisers to choose publishers with hundreds of thousands of visitors per month, most advertisers do not stick with this rule. Many of them allow smaller websites to promote their products.

They may also check the publisher's website if it fits the guidelines that they set. Lastly, they will check the content of the blog. They may decline applications of some websites based on content if it contains dangerous material.

After applying for the program, the next step is to wait for the application to be approved or declined. This usually takes a few days, depending on the diligence of the advertiser to review their applicants and the number of applicants that they get.

If approved, the blogger will be able to see the marketing materials set by the advertiser. These include banner ads, link texts and even videos that can be embedded to your website. Your role as a blogger is to place this in a spot in your website where most of the viewers can find it.

If you are already hosting Google AdSense and other Cost-per-click advertising on your pages, you will have to choose which programs to prioritize for choosing placements. Ideally, you should place the at least one marketing material above the fold. This will ensure that the people viewing your content sees it immediately and it may increase the ad click-through rate.

This brings us to the next step; you will need to find strategies to increase your click-through rate. The click-through rate refers to the number of times that a viewer of the ad clicks on it and goes to the advertiser's website.

After setting up the advertising features of your website, your only problem is how to make people click on them. We will discuss the strategies for increasing the number of clicks on your ads later on in the book.

Shopping/E-commerce Affiliate Networks

Affiliate shopping networks refer to e-commerce websites like Amazon that offer selling opportunities to blogger affiliates. These types of networks are easy to sign up to. For Amazon, for instance, you just need to sign up in their affiliate sign-up page:

https://affiliate-program.amazon.com (US)

You will be asked to provide personal information like your name, age, and country of origin. They will also ask you to provide information about your website like its name, URL and the category where it falls under.

After signing up, you will be asked to complete a tax form. Without a tax form, you will not be allowed to cash your earnings out of Amazon. You can skip this stage for now. However, you need to make sure to take care of this form as your income grows.

After signing up, it may take a few hours to a couple of days for Amazon to review your account. They are pretty lenient with accepting publishers. As long as you are not breaking any law or posting controversial content on your blog, you will probably be accepted.

When you get the acceptance email, you can now post any of the products of that affiliate shopping network on your website. You just need to look for the product that you want to promote, use the embed tool in the header line of your associate account, get the code and paste the code in your website. After a few minutes of posting the code, it should already show the product that you chose.

Affiliate shopping networks give you a wide variety of product to advertise on your blog. Ideally, you should choose a product that will make the blog visitor click on the links you post. Once the visitor is on the advertiser's website, your job is done.

Aside from the variety of products, affiliate shopping networks will also credit the affiliate for all the products bought by the person referred. Let's say you promoted a book in your blog. One of your visitors clicked on the link to the book from your blog and they were redirected to the shopping website.

While in there, they did not buy a book; instead, they bought a new iPhone, phone batteries, and accessories. Even though you did not promote the items bought by the buyer, you will still get paid for the extra items your visitor bought. Even if they bought small cheap items, these profits add up.

The next advantage of becoming an affiliate for a shopping website is that people are usually already familiar with the website and its user interface.

Most people using the internet are already familiar with what Amazon is and how to buy from there. Many of the users who will click on your link already made a purchase from Amazon in the past. Because of this, they are more likely to make a successful purchase from you.

The problem is if the e-commerce website is new. Amazon affiliates can easily earn because their referred visitors already trust Amazon. If you promote a lesser known website, on the other hand, it may take some time for the website to gain the trust of your visitors. In this case, the number of successful sales you make on that website will be less.

Company-level Affiliate Programs

In some cases, a company may choose not to join an affiliate network; instead, they choose to start their own affiliate marketing program with their own coders. This is common in the software and apps market. Software companies usually prefer to maintain their own affiliate program for security reasons and to make sure that all credited sales are valid.

In this type of affiliate marketing platform, you will need to sign up to the company's website to become an affiliate. The process of being accepted is pretty much the same. There will always be a screening process to make sure that all accepted affiliates have a website of good quality.

Once accepted, you will also need to obtain a code that you can post on your website to show the company's marketing materials.

Company level affiliate programs usually use an affiliate marketing campaign management tool or service. These are third party software or online services that make management of campaigns easier. This allows the users to have their own dashboards where they can access the marketing materials, read the news about the latest offers and promotions and track their own sales.

The blogger may also be provided with their own account manager. Account managers are company employees tasked with helping affiliates become successful. They may also create a sense of community among affiliates and facilitate events for affiliates. Think of them as sales managers.

Affiliate marketing is another great tool to maximize the earning potential from your blog. Commonly mistaken for referral marketing, affiliate marketing is a form of marketing known as performance-based marketing, and how it works is a business will reward one or several of its affiliates for each visitor or customer that the affiliates bring in through their own efforts. Bloggers who have been around for a while know that affiliate marketing too has been around for years and they know full well that this form of marketing is one of the most lucrative ways for a blog to earn money online.

Affiliate marketing is one of the oldest forms of marketing around, and one of the most effective methods that benefit the readers while helping your blog make money at the same time. Bloggers make money by building an audience base that stays loyal to the blog by offering products, services or courses that will benefit the audience and help them in a way that they need. Affiliate marketing is merely a faster way to offer products or services without the blogger having to create those products and services from scratch. As a blogger utilizing affiliate marketing, all you have to do is introduce your audience to certain products or services (from companies that you trust and can vouch for regarding effectiveness), and you get a commission on any sales that occur from the marketing efforts on your blog.

Still not convinced how affiliate marketing can help? Five compelling reasons are all you need to see why affiliate marketing is the direction you need to head towards if you are serious about monetizing your blog:

You come to know what your audience really wants, what services or products they are after so you have a better idea of what you may be able to offer in the future should you wish to branch out on your own.

Affiliate marketing monetizes your blog much faster than it would if you were to create your own product from scratch which could take a considerable amount of time depending on what you are offering.

You become known among your readers as a trusted authority, and they become accustomed to buying from you. Provide excellent service and honest reviews, and your readers will have no qualms about buying from you in the future when you someday launch your own products or services.

It is easy to implement. Enough said.

You do not need to be a specialist or an expert to get on board with affiliate marketing, all you need to be is familiar enough with what you are marketing.

How to Maximize Your Earning Potential Through Affiliate Marketing

Ready to start including affiliate marketing as part of your advertising efforts? Take a look at these tips below to help you maximize the earning potential you can get out of your affiliate marketing efforts:

Stick to Your Values – Never compromise your values for the sake of making a quick buck. Always be honest and never give a review that you do not fully believe in yourself if you want to retain credibility among your readers. Yes, affiliate marketing is a great tool to make use of, but only align yourself with products or services that you genuinely love and would recommend to someone else. Ask yourself if you would be willing to refer this product for free, even if you were not being paid for it. If you answer is yes, then go ahead.

Make Honesty Your Best Policy – If your readers feel that they can trust you, they are more likely to stay loyal and buy what you are offering. Never promote a product or service that you do not absolutely love yourself or something that you do not fully believe in. As a blogger who is serious about making an income from your blog, you need to practice transparency all the time and build your reputation around being a credible, reliable and trustworthy source.

Direct Promotion – Instead of promoting your affiliate products or services on the sidebar ads on your blog, consider promoting a product or service directly in a post itself because it garners more attention that way. Include it in a product or service review for example, with as much detail as possible, enough to convince your readers that they should buy the product or service too.

Do not Go Overboard – It is easy to get excited about things that can help you make money, and while it may be tempting to include as many affiliated links on your blog as possible to get the most money out of it, in this instance less may be more. Choose your affiliate links carefully and strategically – this is a much more effective approach than bombarding your blog with dozens of links that are all over the place. Ideally, select affiliates that are in line with the vision and the voice of your blog, your readers will believe an endorsement more if they.

Learn the Ropes – Do not be discouraged by the fact that in affiliate marketing, you are going to have to experiment a little to see what works and what does not. Some may work better than others, but the key is to be persistent until you find what works best for you. Each experience will bring you closer to understanding what your readers want and expect, all of which can prove to be useful information for the future of your blog.

Never Cut Corners – Your relationship with your blog's audience is your most important asset, one that you should never lose. Your readers and your audience are the lifelines of your blog, without them, there is no possibility of maximizing the full earning potential from your blog. Having said that, a blogger should never betray the confidence of their audience and readers for the sake of making money through affiliate marketing, because you risk losing more than just your audience in the long run. Always remind yourself before working on any affiliate marketing efforts that this should improve the relationship between the blog and its readers, not the other way around.

Monetizing Your Blog Through Coaching Services

Contrary to what you may think, you do not have to be blogging for years or to have massive amounts of experience before you can attempt to offer coaching services through your blog. What makes coaching such an in-demand thing is that your readers will inevitably be facing all sorts of challenges at some point in their life. Everyone has their own challenges that he or she need to overcome, and coaching is a positive way to help your readers through that period in his or her lives when they may need it the most. And that is something they would be willing to pay money for.

Coaching is a great tool to use on your blog if you are serious about making money from it. It is common for bloggers to dabble in online coaching these days, and coaching is a great way to nurture a loyal audience following. Why would your audience be keen on coaching services if you were to offer them on your blog? Because of the results that they hope to achieve through that coaching. As a coach, your focus should be on helping your readers to deal with the challenges in their lives positively and constructively to help them overcome the hurdles that they may find impossible to do on their own without a little help.

One of the great things about coaching is the endless possibilities and the many areas that you can delve into. You could opt for life coaching, business coaching, skills coaching, career coaching, performance coaching, executive coaching and much more depending on what you are best at. The most important thing is to convince your readers why your coaching program is better than anyone else's and why they should sign up with you instead.

Why Coaching and How Can It Make Money for My Blog?

Coaching for some is a rewarding experience because they derive pleasure in knowing that they have helped someone else solve a problem or be better at a certain task they were struggling with. Coaching is for some, a way for them to help others and in the process, sharpen their skills at solving a problem while building their reputation as the person to go to if someone were to have a similar problem.

If coaching is something you are great at doing and you already have a blog that has been around long enough to develop a loyal following, take the opportunity to dive into coaching and help make an even bigger impact in the lives of your readers. People are always looking for a solution to their problems and help where they are struggling, and this is something they will be willing to pay for, which makes it a great monetizing opportunity. Coaching on your blog is a great way to strengthen your relationship with your readers who in turn, could draw in more potential readers to your blog which equals more traffic. More traffic at the end of the day means more advertising opportunity, which in turns helps your blog become a money generating machine in the long run that can churn out money for you even while you are sleeping. If your readers like what you are selling, they will buy from you, there is no doubt about that.

Coaching helps your readers, but it also helps you as a blogger at the same time. The whole point of starting a blog in the first place is because you have a passion for something, and a desire to share that information and knowledge (especially if you are an authority on it) with the rest of the world. Coaching is just taking it to the next level where you directly reach out to your readers in an attempt to help them instead of just posting weekly blog posts and updates. Blog posts and articles are speaking to the general audience, but when you offer to coach, suddenly it becomes much more personal. Additionally, if your readers already like what they have seen on your blog thus far, they will not hesitate to pay for any coaching programs you offer if they feel they stand to benefit from it.

The best part about coaching through your blog? Your earnings are not limited by your geographical location. Because it is online, you have the potential to reach people from across the globe, which means your earning potential skyrockets just like that. If you are good, people will be willing to pay.

How to Get Started with Coaching on Your Blog

The first thing you need to do if you want to offer to coach on your blog is to establish the niche you are coaching for. A coaching program that a reader is going to be most enticed towards is one that highlights the aspects of a situation that the reader is going through and that they need help with. To do that, the coaching program offered on your blog needs to be specialized in solving specific problems that your readers have, only then will they be willing to pay money for your program.

The second thing you need to do to establish a successful coaching program that is going to help you generate an income from your blog is to identify what kind of coaching structure you are going to go for. Are your sessions going to be solely blog based? Would you offer a live video session on your blog that your readers can tune into? Would you be holding your coaching sessions in person in a specific location? Either method you choose, your readers should only be able to sign up for your coaching sessions through your blog, as that is how you will be able to generate an income from it. Coaching through your blog would definitely be the easier option as all your readers would need is a good internet connection. They do not have to waste time commuting back and forth, do not have to sit in traffic and they have the flexibility of tuning in to your coaching sessions when it is convenient for them.

Create a coaching program that is ongoing, so your readers will always keep coming back to your blog. An ongoing coaching series has a lot more earning potential than a one-off program. Remember to make your coaching sessions educational, informative, inspirational, and most importantly, offer insightful tips that your readers can employ to their own problems. Create content that is of value to your readers to keep them coming back for more. Teach your readers how to achieve their goals and overcome challenges with constructive tools and advice and your coaching courses will become a hit in no time.

The Importance of Content Delivery

By now, you should have already come to realize that the success of a blog boils down to the kind of content that is delivered on the blog. For a blog to succeed enough to the level that it can constantly make money, it needs to always be at the top of its game when it comes to content, and mediocre or lackluster content is just not going to cut it. A successful blog is one that delivers content of value to its readers.

The Right Way to Deliver Content on Your Blog for Maximum Earning Potential

Bloggers who make some serious dough with their blogs know the five golden rules when it comes to the kind of content they have on their blog. So, how do you always ensure that the content on your blog is top-notch enough for your blog to become a money generating machine?

By Being Yourself – Never try to be someone that you are not. A blog that is trying to pretend to be something that it is not is a blog that is never going to get very far, much less make any money from. Remember the reason that you decided to start your blog in the first place - because you have insight, knowledge, or skills that you know could be useful to other people and you want to share that with the world. So do it! Do not try to copy or imitate other successful blogs because no two blogs are the same. Make your blog your own, be your own person and your content will have a unique voice of its own that is going to resonate with the readers.

By Not Being Fake – Starting a blog should not be just about making money, you need also to be passionate and love what you are doing if you are going to deliver content of quality. Content that isn't genuine is going to just turn your readers away if they feel that your blog is not genuine enough for them. Loss of audience equals loss of revenue, so if you are going to start a blog, be sure that it is also about the passion and not just about the money. Do what you love, and the money will follow.

By Being Engaging – The content on your blog should be of an interactive nature, where it encourages your readers to respond with their own comments and reach out to you via the email address listed on your blog. Be an authority that your readers want to reach out for advice and input after reading your blog. Post a variety of different things, share personal experiences, talk about topics from your own point of view, anything that you think will be able to engage your readers just a little bit more.

By Being Confident – To post content that is worthy and valuable on your blog, you are going to have to be confident about what you are writing about. Do not compare yourself to other writers or bloggers who may seem to post funnier content or content with a more creative flair and style for writing, for example. Constant comparisons and trying to keep up with other bloggers will only serve to make you lose sight of what unique traits you have to offer on your blog, and your content will inevitably suffer because of it. Be confident about what you have to share and let it show in the way you deliver your content, and your audience will respond well to that.

Be Settling for Nothing Less Than Perfection – The content on your blog is going to be out there for the world to see. And you are going to want to make sure that what they are seeing is nothing short of perfect. As a blogger, you should always be working and striving to improve, not just on your skills as a writer, but in the way you deliver the content before hitting the publish button. Read your post several times over, check for any grammar or spelling errors, eye your content from a critical point of view and ask yourself how this post is going to add value to the person who is reading it. Settle for nothing less than perfect.

Monetizing Through Sponsored Posts

Sponsored posts are one of the quickest methods of making money from your blog. Sponsored content is content that you are being paid to write or come up with by a company or a brand, which means that the content you create will have to be promoting a particular brand or service offered by the company in question. Sponsored content differentiates itself from marketing through one simple aspect — you are paid for the content you create, as opposed to relying on possibly generating an income based on the number of clicks or sales.

Introducing your readers to new products or services that they may not already be aware of is one way of providing value to your readers, but the trick is here to create content that is top-notch and honest at the same time without compromising the credibility of your blog.

When it comes to sponsored posts, you may be tempted to take on as many as possible because you are guaranteed a payment for each one, but cool your jets and try to avoid doing so, because a blog that has too many sponsored brands can be a turn off for a lot of readers. They will begin to doubt if they can really trust what your blog is saying if they feel you are just creating these sponsored posts for the sake of the money. Be savvy and be smart and selective about the kind of sponsored posts and campaigns you want to take on and limit the number of brands you commit to at any given time. Even though your content is being paid for by the sponsor for you to spin some positive light on it, it should still hold a genuine voice to it and not come across as fake to your readers. Before you hit the publish button, ask yourself - if you were reading your post from a third-party point of view, would it be convincing enough?

What Is the Earning Potential with Sponsored Content?

You need to know what your blog is worth. Earnings from a sponsored post can vary depending on the company and brand in question, but it is also important for you as a blogger to know what the value of your blog is. If your blog has been around for a long time, for example, and has developed a strong following with hits on the site every day, you have more bargaining power which will allow you to negotiate a better deal for your sponsored content.

Why Sponsored Posts Are an Awesome Revenue Generating Tool

With the rise of influencers online, companies realize the value of purchasing sponsored posts and are constantly on the lookout for influencers and bloggers to work with. Having a company featured on a blog is a great way to boost sales, and for this reason, it is a great way for bloggers to take this opportunity to make some money if they have a blog space to offer.

What makes sponsored posts so great is that you do not have to invest too much time or effort into it. In fact, it is quite possibly easier than a lot of other types of campaigns which can be more demanding and cost a lot more money. Sponsored posts are easy. In fact, sometimes all a company needs is a link or a mention of their product or service on existing blog posts or an upcoming blog post that they could pay to be mentioned in.

In contrast with affiliate marketing, one of the most exciting things about sponsored posts for bloggers is that they are paid more or less immediately. This may vary depending on the sponsor in question, of course, as some sponsors will prefer to pay up front and others may opt for payment only after you have published a post on them. Still, it is a lot faster than affiliate marketing and advertising, and the pay here can be pretty good depending on how popular your blog may be and how much traffic it generates on a daily basis. It is a quicker option to monetizing your blog compared to a lot of other monetizing efforts.

How to Secure Sponsored Posts on Your Blog

If you do not already have companies who are queuing up to get sponsored on your blog, then you need to be proactive and start approaching companies that you would like to work with and convince them why it would be a great idea to collaborate with your blog. If you are worried about whether your blog needs to be amazingly popular or have a high volume of traffic before companies and brands will even consider working with you, don't worry. As long as you can produce great content of value, that is going to be what matters the most.

When presenting your pitch to these companies, be specific about what the company or brand can expect if they decide to work with you. Tell them your ideas with enthusiasm and give them as much detail as possible to really show it is going to be well worth their time and money to secure a sponsored post on your blog. Tell them what you plan to write, who your readers are and what they want, how much traffic your blog generates, be as specific as possible and spare no detail.

Do not be afraid to show your creativity when trying to convince companies and brands to work with your blog. Creativity shows that you think outside the box and you are all about ideas. It is ideas with a creative spark that is going to drive an interest towards a product or service. Show the companies or brands that you hope to work with what you can do for them, and they will be more than interested in teaming up with your blog for a sponsored post or two. Maybe even more.

The Types of Sponsored Post Options to Work With

The types of sponsored post options that bloggers would have to work with are sponsored posts that have access to the readers and sponsored posts which are just a link to the blog or website. The type of sponsored content would depend on the company or brand's preference and what they think would work best for them.

Sponsored content that has access to readers would depend on the type of influence your blog has. The more influence a blog has, the more likely the company is to decide on this route when it comes to post sponsorship. Sponsored content that works with just a link would depend on how much authority a blog's domain has. The higher the domain authority, the more opportunities your blog will have. Which is why it is important to pitch as many details as possible about your blog to the company or brand you hope to work with so they can make an informed decision and get the most out of their sponsored post collaboration with your blog.

Monetizing Through Product Creation

Aside from earning money through advertising, make the most out of your blog by offering products and services that your readers will not be able to score elsewhere. When a product or service is offered exclusively, your earning potential increases because readers will only have to come to your blog to get what they want. Even better if you are an authority in your field and they know that what they are paying for is going to add value and be well worth it. An example of how to make the most money out of your blog would be through creating and selling online courses, selling products or services, and organizing giveaways.

Creating and Selling Online Courses

The first question you may ask is, why would readers pay for an online course? One reason – because the course is teaching them something they need to know. And let's face it, online learning is big these days, thanks in large part to how convenient it is to learn something from the comforts of home and at your own pace. If you are an expert on a subject, consider creating an online course on your blog.

When creating an online course, it is best to focus on a specific subject or topic at any given time. Online courses hold more value than your average blog posts because of the teaching quality involved, and the opportunity your readers are getting to learn something of value that they could make use of for the money that they are paying.

To successfully create an online course that is going to help generate income for your blog, you would want to keep these helpful pointers in mind:

Include the Two "I"s in Your Course – The two "I"s, in this case, would be informative and inspirational. This is the most important criteria that you are going to need to encompass into your blog. Otherwise, you would just be wasting everyone's time, and your readers are going to become disenchanted with your blog. Share information that is based on facts, and create a course that is going to inspire your readers into action once the course is over. Being informational will set your blog apart because your readers will come to know that your blog is the one to go to if they want to learn something useful. Being inspirational with your posts, ideas and sharing personal experiences, which you can incorporate into your course, will inspire your readers into believing that they can do it too.

Be Clear with Your Objectives and Focus – If you intend to monetize your blog, this is another big factor you are going to want to pay attention to. If you can create a course that is niche, focused and targeted to a specific group where there is a demand, that immediately increases your chances of monetization right there. You need to offer a course that makes your readers feel they NEED to be a part of this or they will be missing out on something important. That they NEED your course because it holds the answers to everything they need to know.

Price Your Course Reasonably – Everyone wants to make as much money as they possibly can, but let's not get carried away here. To really draw your audience in, you are going to need to offer a course that is fair enough to compensate for your time and effort, but at the same time not priced too high that your target audience is going to feel it is way out of their budget and price range to take part in the course. If you can offer the course at a discount, especially if it is your first online course, that would be even better.

Selling Products, Services and Organizing Giveaways

If you have a passion or skill for something, consider offering that service, skill or product on your blog. Selling a skill, service, or product that your readers need will cement your blog's reputation as the go-to blog for what they need. This is turn will drive a higher volume of traffic towards your blog which helps with the advertising aspect of it, so really it is a beneficial situation on many levels.

Giveaways are also another method of generating an income from your blog. Depending on the nature of your blog, research some companies that you can potentially work with, approach them and see if they would be interested in a product giveaway collaboration with your blog. If you are a beauty blog for example, and you have posted about reviews about your favorite makeup or skincare brands on your blog, consider approaching those companies for a possible opportunity. Convincing companies to collaborate with you on your blog is not as hard as it may seem, the key is to convince them why it would benefit their company to be working with you.

Selling products, services, and organizing giveaways are a great way to generate traffic to your website and if your readers like what you are pitching, they are more likely to buy from you, and keep revisiting your blog many times over.

The rise of the information product is in direct correlation to the rise of pro bloggers, and is a great way to monetize your blog without relying on anybody else. Being totally in control of the content and final outcome of a product is why I'm such a big fan of the information product. While affiliate partnering is great (we'll get to that later), why sell other people's products all the time when you could be selling your own? More kudos? Check. More job satisfaction? Check. A bigger piece of the financial pie? Check!

But how to begin?

Research

The subject of your information product should be something you consider yourself an expert in and enjoy researching and writing about. Think about what you can offer people who are already interested in reading your travel posts and test it out on them first. Do people respond well to the money-saving backpacking tips you offer? Are your readers more interested in guides to a certain part of the world perhaps?

In this instance it may be necessary to ask your readers directly what they would actually buy from you. If you already have an [email list](#) of subscribers to your blog, devise a survey with a fun company like www.surveymonkey.com and ask them to fill it in. Write a blog post about it and share your survey link across your burgeoning social media networks. You don't need a lot of responses to start identifying ideas and patterns amidst your market and start creating a bundle of highly valuable information to sell on your blog.

Depending on the results of your research, this may be a guide to traveling with children in South America or a video series on how to get a job teaching English in China. The main thing is that you know and love your niche topic, that people have told you they want more of it from you and that you create something of real value that they can't get from anyone else.

Writing, formatting and design

After you've researched enough to find the cross-over between what people want from you and what you know and love enough to write expertly about, it's time to actually sit down write the thing. Even if your chosen medium is a video course you'll still need to get a script down, so this stage cannot be avoided.

The best way I've found to fit in any new project around my other commitments is to get up an hour earlier and work on it before I start my day. I'm really, really not a morning person but this way, no matter what happens throughout the day, the creation stage is happening – bit by bit, day by day.

Depending on how you like to work you can either set a goal of, say, a thousand words a day, or set a timer to go off and write as much as you can in the hour. Either way, write and don't stop until you have your first draft completed. Only then should you go back and self-edit. Then proofread. Then send it off to somebody to do a copy edit. Then get a professional to give it a final proofread. Phew. I know, right? But this is what it takes. The point is to put in all the hard work now to enable you to build a residual income from your information product for many years to come.

The design and creation of your information product can be outsourced to a professional on a freelancing site like People Per Hour, as can the copy editing and proofreading stages (which should never be skipped just because you consider yourself a good writer by the way).

In my experience, and that of most successful bloggers I talk to, it's best not to get too bogged down with trying to do absolutely everything. Write the thing yourself, then outsource the rest of the work to somebody who excels in the area of expertise you need. Outsourcing the design and proofreading stages might cost you a few bucks to begin with but being professional will pay off, plus you can spend the time you save doing what you do best – travel blogging! You're a travel blogger so your job is to write and market your product. Speaking of which...

Marketing

The main thing you'll need to focus on after the writing stage is marketing the heck out of your product. You'll need to 'launch' it properly and develop a marketing strategy to get your product out there to the masses.

You need to get yourself, your blog and your new product out there and get people to really sit up and take note of all the amazing benefits it will bring them.

Use social media to reach your biggest fans and to create new ones. Don't push the thing on people but present it to them in such a way that they understand all the benefits and amazing value it can provide them with. Marketing your own product can sometimes feel overwhelming, as it seems there are so many options to consider.

To help you out, below are some free ways to market a new product, guide or eBook:

Give away free copies to a certain number of your blog's email subscribers before the official launch date and ask them to spread the word (plus email you with any comments or suggestions for improvement).

Ask anybody who may have contributed to the creation of your information product to blog and/or post about it on social media.

Contact other relevant bloggers and local journalists with a free copy and ask them to review your product (don't forget to mention why your product is so useful and relevant to their readers).

Send out press releases, both online and manually, to any relevant journalists you can get contact details for (the local press tend to pick up on these things a lot more than the nationals).

Email all your friends, your family and your extended network announcing your new venture and ask them to spread the word by email, word of mouth and on their social media networks.

Ask any readers, friends and family that have pre-launch copies to send you short reviews and testimonials and include the best of them on the product sales page of your blog.

Use [Google Keyword Planner](#) to discover the phrases your target readers are using to search for related information online. Then write articles including these phrases and publish them on free but popular article sites, like [Ezine Articles](#) and [Hubpages](#).

Create a trailer introducing your new product and upload it to YouTube.

These are just the free ideas of course – there's also Facebook, Google and other advertising and promotion to think about. That type of marketing depends on you having a budget though, and this book is about how to make money from travel blogging – not how to spend it.

So what did we learn on our travels?

The great thing about launching your own information product is that once all the hard work is done it's pure profit for you – no middle-man costs (apart from perhaps PayPal fees). It is a lot of hard work in the initial stages though, and you'll need to work hard to establish a large (or at least fiercely loyal) readership before you can launch an information product and expect it to sell. In the end though, if you can go on to reap the rewards of all your hard work in years to come with only the lightest of marketing efforts, it will all be worthwhile.

Secrets for Curating and Rewriting Great Content

We know by know what a difference wow content and attention grabbing headlines can make when it comes to developing a seriously profitable blog. However, how do you constantly come up with power-packed content that interests and impact readers?

Fret not, I have your back there. I am spilling all the beans about digging out super powered content that has the potential to make your blog massively successful.

Content creation

While content creation is about creating a piece of content (blog post, video, image or more) from scratch, creation is about gathering already existing content such as blog posts, social media updates or eBooks that are relevant to your niche, and sharing them with your readers/followers.

Several surveys have revealed that the number one challenge for blog owners or content marketers is to come up with sufficient quality content to build a more engaged social media audience and populate their blogs with top notch content.

Though it has its share of limitations, content creation has the following benefits:

- It helps build relationships with other bloggers and influencers. Content creation is like a brilliant synergy where everyone benefits from giving each other a larger audience. It helps build some amazing online partnerships with industry influencers.

- According to a Crowdtap study, 44% of industry experts work with other brands since it offers them a relevant opportunity for their audience, too.

- Content creation saves time. If you are operating multiple blogs and social media channels, and do not have the time to populate each of them with stellar content on a daily basis, content creation is like manna from heaven for your blog.

- Admit it. You cannot be a pro at everything. Content creation helps you fill the gaps that you may have left as a creator. Sourcing content from diverse, reputable channels gives you the advantage of bringing more variety to your content.

- Having said that, ensure that if you use content from other sources, link attribution is given to the writer and blog page. Seek proper permissions before using someone else's content. Ensure that the terms are clear before posting, so there's no confusion or legal hassles later.

Have you heard about Upworthy? Yes, the same viral site that posts interesting content with catchy, clickbait style headlines.

When they launched, they became a roaring success only by repackaging and curating a majority of their content from other sources and posting it using sexy and shocking headlines. They eventually transitioned into content creation, but a lot of the early success was their ability to repackage promising content from varied sources and presenting it in a more stunning, attention-grabbing style.

4 Ways for Finding Great Content in Your Niche

1. Go to a BuzzSumo. Enter your topic or domain in the search option, and click go. You will be presented with the most popular content related to your topic, including statistics such as numbers of social media shares and pages that link back to it.

2. Google Trends is another great place for digging out great content based on organic searches. So, if you want to have a nice combination of content that is popular on both social media and search engines, include Google Trends into your content creation strategy. You will see an entire list of trending stories for the last 24 hours. Enter a specific topic if you want to gauge the changing popularity of a topic and the interest it generates among readers of varied geographic regions.

3. A lot of viral sites pick up their content from aggregators such as Reddit. It is indeed the "Front Page of the Internet" as it describes itself. There's a goldmine of hidden content in subreddits on virtually any topic under the sun.

4. Unlike other content aggregation channels, Reddit's content is ranked by freshness and popularity score, which makes it an ideal platform for digging out trending content, especially about lesser known niches.

On signing up, a user automatically has access to a a large amount of content. You have to manually unsubscribe from subreddits that aren't of any interest to you. There's plenty of opportunity to get your hands on little known, detailed, multiperspective and information-rich content.

Use the power of question and answer sites. Quora is another great place for finding informative and detailed content presented as answers to a query by most experts in their fields. So you may have skin experts offering the best home remedies for black heads or a practicing Stoic sharing his insightful beliefs about the philosophy of Stoicism.

There are other question and answer sites such as Wiki Answers, How Stuff Works and Yahoo Answers, where you can unearth a lot of interesting stuff related to your niche.

5 Stellar Tips Used by Professionals for Rewriting Existing Content

Rewriting has gained a sort of notoriety on the online content world owing to the misconceptions people hold about it. It is not simply altering a few words or inserting a few synonymous to make it appear original.

Rewriting content is about repackaging existing content to lend it a fresh appeal, while still retaining the essence of the original.

If you already have a large bank of blog posts or original content, it is easy to repurpose it into newer and fresher pieces of content instead of starting from scratch and hitting a roadblock. Cut your time by using these valuable strategies for repurposing existing pieces into stellar content.

- Transform lists into standalone content pieces. If you have several list-based posts such as "7 crackling smart investment options" and other similar posts, you can very well convert it into individual blog posts. Each investment option can be turned into a separate blog post by listing its features, merits, and demerits. Fleshing out each point also gives your readers more detailed and insightful information.

- It gives you an opportunity to build on or expand existing ideas by conducting research. Repacking lists into individual articles also establishes your expertise in a specific subject. Add a few case studies or examples to make the posts more comprehensive and interesting to read.

- Combine multiple posts into a summary post. You may have written multiple blog posts about child psychology or about improving learning and development among children. Use key point from each blog to create a summary blog post like "Top Tips for Improving Your Child's Learning Abilities" or "5 Important Things Parents Must Know About Development Learning." It is actually just the opposite of the first tip.

- Revamp old posts for a brand new audience. You may have written something keeping in mind a specific audience. For instance, operational challenges faced by nonprofit organizations. You may want to cater to another type of audience; for instance, small business owners. While the general framework will remain similar, you will have to tweak a few points to suit profit organizations. This will help you target different sets of audience in a more focused manner with almost similar content.

- Update existing posts with latest information. In today's fast paced world, things change at the blink of an eyelid. There are forever new developments and updates, especially in the world of internet marketing and technology. The blog post you drafted a couple of years ago may be relevant, but there may be newer trends and developments that you readers may want to know.

- For instance, if you wrote a post about best SEO practices for bloggers in 2015, you may want to update it by including newer SEO dynamics and trends that held relevance over the past year. Make it a practice to review old blog posts periodically to gauge if they can be updated with fresh statistics, newer examples/case studies or important recent developments. Google and other search engines love fresh, updated and time-relevant content.

- Focus on ideas, not words. Even the most seasoned writers and bloggers fall into the trap of copying words above ideas. Do not restructure the content sentence by sentence or even paragraph by paragraph just because you are rewriting an existing piece of content. Instead of focusing on expressions and composition of the original writer, try and concentrate on ideas. Rewriting is not about shuffling a few words and sentences. The objective is to understand what exactly is being conveyed, and then communicate it in your own, distinct style.

- Add fresh, new ideas. Yes, we can all have our Eureka moments while writing, where we think of something fresh and exciting that hasn't been covered by the original writer or our original post. Utilize this moment of epiphany to the fullest, and include these new insights into your post. You may want to include an interesting piece of research or share an example or add your own unique perspective on the matter.

- No rule says one cannot include a fresh element to rewritten content. Do not be afraid to reinvent and improve the post with newer insights. It will only help in making the article appear fresher and more distinct from the original.

- Re-writing headlines. Alerting the headline to give your post a new angle is the easiest way to begin the rewriting process. Find something that is still relevant to your post but lends it a slightly diverse perspective or angle. You may also want to include a different keyword or optimize the post for Google or social media channels.

- Make the introductory paragraph unique. The opening paragraph is your chance to grab the interest of your competitor or send them running to competitors. Make it an enticing proposition by including something of value that does not feature in the original article. It can be anything from a statistic to a new piece of research to an attention-grabbing pro tip. Give readers a strong reason to read further even if they have read the original post. Avoid fluff in the opening paragraph (or anywhere in the post).

- Another neat tip is to reinvent the layout of your post by including different headings and subheadings. You may want to expand the article by breaking it into sub headings if there aren't any in the original. It will also make your piece more scan-able and readable.

- Finding Jaw Dropping Beautiful Images

- Images are an important component of your blog profit strategy. They complement your written words to create a more wholesome experience for the reader. All top blogs use attention grabbing images to communicate their message compellingly. Using the right images also boost your search engine optimization efforts.

So how to do you find images that make your blog posts look amazing? Here are some expert tips to find the perfect images for your post.

Take Pictures Yourself

This really saves you the trouble of finding the perfect and most relevant images for your blog. There are no hassles about seeking permissions, paying for high-quality stock photos or digging into the creative commons public domain.

If you are writing a post and have a fair idea about how to represent it best visually, use you a camera or your smartphone to take high-quality pictures. Ensure they are well-lit to make them appear high-resolution images. Go outdoors and take pictures in bright light to make them look more flattering.

Paid Royalty-Free Stock Images

If you have a higher budget, you can buy royalty free images from iStockPhoto or Shutterstock. They have a huge assortment of images for virtually any conceivable topic under the sun.

Bloggers/publishers have the option of paying a one-time fee for using an image several times for various purposes (without any fixed time limit for using it) or sign up for a monthly/yearly subscription that allows you to download a fixed number of images per month/year.

These photographs are high vector images that make your site look professional, and save you from getting into any copyright trouble later.

Free Photo Resources

There are many sites such as Pixabay, Pexels, Unsplash and more where you can get access to a whole bunch of high-quality and on-topic images. Simply enter a few keywords related to the picture in the search option and pick the ones that fit well with your post. Pixabay has a fairly good collection of images, which can be used even for commercial purposes without attribution.

Just ensure that you do not use the sponsored images that show at the top of your search since these are the pay to use images. It is fairly easy to tell because the sponsored images have a distinct watermark.

Ensure you read the terms of every picture you are using very carefully to avoid getting into copyright issues trouble. Some pictures may require an attribution (credit to the owner), some may not.

Even though the prospect of using free images seems lucrative, things change pretty rapidly in the online business world. You never know when the original owner of the image may change its terms of use.

You may not have a large budget in the initial stages of your blog, which makes these free resources a good place, to begin with. Once you start raking in some profits, it is a good idea to invest in royalty-free paid stock images.

Others Blogs and Pages

You cannot simply get images from other people's blogs and pages by performing a simple Google image search. It could lead to serious copyright violations and legal trouble.

If you really like a particular image that's on another blog, begin by complimenting the owner/photo and seek their permission clearly for using the photo. Always seek permission before posting the image and proceed only when you have documented permission stating their consent for using their original work on your blog.

Give them proper credit by mentioning them as the source and linking back to their page or website below the image.

Creative Commons License (CC)

Images under the Creative Commons license are in public domain, which means you are free to use, reuse and distribute them. Depending on individual Creative Commons (CC) licenses, users can use images for commercial purposes or create derivatives of the image.

There are several CC licenses, which means you have to carefully go through the license of each image to know what is permissible under the specific license. To be on the safer side, always attribute all images under the Creative Commons license to their rightful owner.

Wikimedia Commons and Flickr are some great sources for finding CC licensed images. Again while using images from these sources check all licenses by clicking on the individual terms of use/some rights reserved link. You will learn the terms of use of that particular photo such as, whether it can be shared, adapted and used commercially. Also, it will be mentioned if an attribution link to the owner of the image is required.

Here's a quick breakdown of various Creative Commons Licenses

Attribution: This means that the user is required to attribute the image to its original owner in the specified manner. You also have to be mindful of the fact that the image should not be used in a manner which implies that the owner of the image endorses your page/brand or you in any way.

Share-Alike: This clause means the image should not be held under different or restrictive terms than those laid down by the original creator.

Non Commercial: The image should only be utilized for non-commercial purposes.

No Derivative Works: The image is to be used only as it is without altering it or creating derivatives of it.

9 Kick-Ass Resources to Enhance Your Content Writing from Good to Wow

Of course, you have great content and the best formats to present it. However, the tools listed below can expedite the process or make it even more effective. Here are five resources that should be in the tool box of every content creator or marketer.

1. Grammarly

This is really your must have tool when it comes to writing grammatically correct and smooth flowing blogs. The software helps scan your text for any grammatical, punctuation and spelling errors really fast, thus making it appear professional. As a resource, it gives more direction and clarity to your writing. It helps optimize your post and makes it easier to read.

2. Hemingway

Hemingway is a virtual editing tool that is hugely popular among content writers, with good reason. It is a user-friendly text editing software, which highlights complex sentences and offers suggestions for eliminating unwanted adverbs. It also converts drab reading passive sentences into a more actionable active voice.

There is a tracker, which shows you the final count of words, characters, and paragraphs. You can fine-tune the text structure to make it more appealing and readable. Once you are finish making changes, the file can be exported in an .html format.

3. Ideaflip

As a content creator, learn to develop ideas rather than working on the first one that strikes you. Brainstorming is integral to the process of creating wow-worthy content, and Ideaflip helps you do that.

Instead of writing everything on a piece of paper, use Ideaflip. It offers a highly visual, dynamic and interactive platform for developing ideas.

4. Power Thesaurus

Power Thesaurus is a crowdsourced app that does not have any ads (yay!). It is a hit with writers for its elegant interface and streamlined search options. The app is always updated with the newest linguistic trends, which makes it a must-have ammo in your writer warfare kit.

5. Ahrefs

Ahrefs is several SEO resources that can push your blog content into the next league by ranking higher on search engines. Some tools help you keep a close eye on your competitors' SEO tactics and enhance your own content.

6. Canva

We have discussed the power of using compelling visuals in drawing people to your blog. Canva helps you accomplish that goal, with its aesthetically pleasant layouts and high utility value. Use it when you want to add some sparkle to your visual content. It allows graphically challenged folks to create professional and stunning looking visual presentations, infographics and social media cover images. They have a wide assortment of templates that can be adapted for any niche.

7. StackEdit

StackEdit is a handy tool for converting text files into .html or exporting them from Google Docs or Word without altering the formatting. It is an inbuilt browser mark-down that has a ton of great features such as shortcuts that make your writing more unique, has a variety of themes and several layouts. Also, the spell checker is compatible with several languages. The best part? StackEdit can be synced with a variety of tools such as WordPress and Dropbox. It is also available for offline use.

9. Yoast WordPress Plugin

Even though you do not have to stuff your posts with a bunch of keywords, you still have to make your posts more searchable for readers. What's the point of writing phenomenal blog posts when your readers are not able to find them?

Yoast lets you know how optimized your content is regarding a specific keyword and content analysis. It offers tons of helpful suggestions about how to optimize your post to please search engines and readers. It also includes a handy site map feature, which boosts your search engine page indexing efforts.

Content Scheduling

A well-organized and comprehensive content schedule allows you to stay on track with your editorial goals. It helps you save time, and take on multiple tasks, while still running your blog on auto-pilot. Here are some power-packed content scheduling tips.

1. Have a clear brand/blog persona and start by brainstorming content that matches your persona. The content should address your target audience's most pressing issues. Aspire to be a trusted and respected source of information related to the industry.

2. Plenty of marketers test their content on social media before creating full-fledged blog posts about the same. The experimental post can be thought-provoking, fresh, engaging, humorous and exclusive. Gauge if your content has the potential to be popular on social media.

3. Create a content calendar for 1 to 3 months in advance, and keep adding to it. Bigger events such as Q&A's, interviews, eBooks, product releases, conferences, podcasts, live videos can be announced once a date is locked.

4. Social media posts are best scheduled in advance unless you want to post about recent developments.

5. As a good practice, create 3-4 long blog posts a week, a couple of SlideShare presentations, syndication on sites such Tumblr, 4-5 daily comments from influencers around the web, an infographic every two weeks and a monthly eBook.

6. Google Calendar is a great resource for planning and scheduling content.

7. Keep a close eye on trends too. You may be the most fastidious planner, but you can never completely rely on scheduled content. Keep a close eye on latest trends for cashing in on latest stories. Monitor your content analytics closely. Your content calendar will keep evolving according to your readers' response.

If it is not working for you, try different types of content. Look around at what competitors are doing in a dynamic and ever-changing world of content marketing.

How to Schedule Posts on WordPress

For publishing posts to your audience's time zone, go to the WordPress dashboard and head to settings. Tap on the General Menu option. Select the appropriate time zone and click "Save Changes."

There is a "Publish meta box" on the right-hand corner of the "Edit" option adjacent to the Publish button. Set the date and time the date you wish to publish your post.

Schedule you blog post at the given date and time. Tap on the "Schedule" button.

For rescheduling posts, select "Edit" adjacent to the right-hand side of the Schedule tab. Set the new date and time for publishing the post and update it.

The same process can be used for re-publishing posts that were previously published at a given date and time. You can also create a new post and make it appear as if it was published earlier by following the same process. There are lots WordPress plugins for scheduling posts, too.

Good luck, go out there and make a Money Making Blog!

Be sure to give us your comments and what you think of our book on Amazon.

We hope you have found our book educational. Please visit our website at www.underpaidoverworked.com

If you like this book, please check out: Starting from Nothing: How to Develop an Internet Marketing Campaign.

www.ingramcontent.com/pod-product-compliance
Lightning Source LLC
Chambersburg PA
CBHW030950240526
45463CB00016B/2329